Going places available in hardback
People at work
How places change
Finding the way
People on holiday

Going places available in paperback
Town and countryside
Where people shop
People on the move
People at work

Acknowledgements

Illustrations by Steve Cox
Photographs by Zul Mukhida except for: pp. 8, 9, 19t Jenny Matthews;
pp. 14t Tim Garrod; 14b Jayne Knights; 15m Oliver Cockell; 15bl Tim
Richardson; 15br John Heinrick; 19b Tim Richardson, Zul Colour Library;
p. 24t Ian Harwood; 24b Nick Hawkes, Ecoscene; p. 25b D. Parker,
Tropix; p. 27 Art Directors

The author and publisher would like to thank the staff and pupils
of Balfour Infant School, Brighton.

A CIP catalogue record for this book is available from
the British Library.

ISBN 0-7136-5939-4

First paperback edition published 2001
First published in hardback in 1994 by
A & C Black (Publishers) Ltd
37 Soho Square, London, W1D 3QZ
© 1994 A & C Black (Publishers) Ltd

A CIP record for this book is available from
the British Library.

Typeset in Rowland Phototypesetting Ltd,
Bury St Edmunds, Suffolk
Printed in Belgium by Proost International Book Production

going places

Where people shop

Barbara Taylor

Illustrations by Steve Cox

Photographs by Zul Mukhida and Jenny Matthews

Contents

A & C Black · London

Going shopping

Do you help with the shopping? Are the shops near to your home or a long way away? Do you go to lots of small shops or a few big shops?

Ask your friends about the shops they have visited this week.

I went on the bus with dad to the toy shop in town.

I went in the car with my mum to the supermarket.

I went with my brother to the grocer's at the end of our road.

You could draw a chart like this one to show what you find out. Which sort of shop did most children visit?

Basket 1

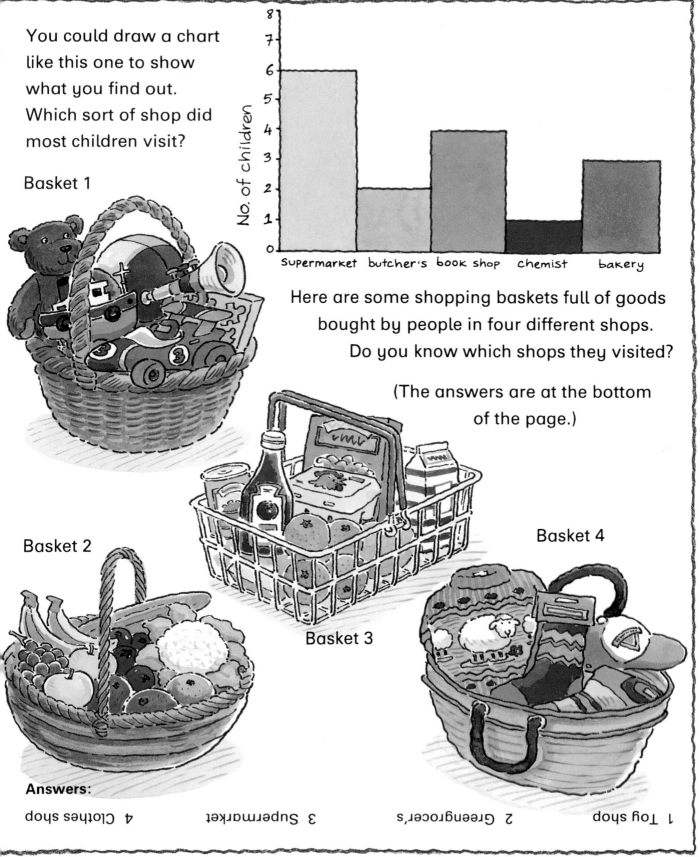

No. of children

8
7
6
5
4
3
2
1
0

supermarket   butcher's   book shop   chemist   bakery

Here are some shopping baskets full of goods bought by people in four different shops. Do you know which shops they visited?

(The answers are at the bottom of the page.)

Basket 4

Basket 2

Basket 3

Answers:

Trading

Have you ever given a friend one thing, such as a sticker or an apple, in return for something else? Shopping first started with people swapping things like this.

It's a deal!

I'll swap my ball for your fishing net.

People who were good at growing or making one thing swapped it for something else which they could not easily grow or make. This is called trading or bartering.

But swapping goods had its problems. What if your goods weren't very easy to transport? Or maybe you needed to buy something in the spring, but your crops weren't ready to swap until the autumn?

So, people began to use money as a way of paying for goods. It wasn't like the money we use today. Shells, beads, grain and pieces of silver have all been used as money in the past.

cowrie shells

beads

grain

early coins

Soon traders began to travel to other countries to exchange or buy goods. They came back with new goods and exciting inventions from all over the world. As more traders travelled about, they followed the same routes from place to place. These were called trade routes.

This picture shows Arab traders travelling by sea.

Markets

The earliest kind of shops were markets where traders gathered together to swap their goods with one another. Goods weren't measured very accurately; they were sold by the cupful, handful or cartload. Often people argued over the price of the goods and tried to get them more cheaply.

This picture shows a vegetable market in Italy in the 15th century.

A modern British market.

Have you got a market near you? How often is the market held? What do the stalls sell? Are any of the goods made or grown by the people selling them?

How is your local market different from the ones in these pictures? Can you see what the people are selling?

Bolivia

Thailand

Morocco

Shops today

Nowadays, we don't usually buy things from the people who made them. Instead, the people who make the goods, the manufacturers, sell them to people called wholesalers. The wholesalers sell the goods to lots of different shops. Most shops sell a whole range of goods which have been made by lots of different manufacturers.

These pictures show how a batch of teddy bears gets to the shops. The money made from the sale of the teddy bears is split between the shopkeeper, the wholesaler and the manufacturer.

1 The manufacturer makes the teddy bears.

3 The wholesaler sells the teddy bears to different shops.

2 The wholesaler buys the teddy bears from the manufacturer.

4 Mrs Smith buys one of the teddy bears from a shop.

13

Big shops, small shops

How many different kinds of shops do you have in your local area? Do you have any small shops like the one in the picture on the right? Do you ever go to a big supermarket like the one in the picture below? How is a supermarket different from a small local shop? Here are some of the things you could find out about.

Do the shops have different opening hours?

Do they sell different things?

Is the price of the food the same?

Are there any special offers?

Are the shops easy to get to?

You could carry out a survey to find out which shops people like best.

Imagine that a new department store has been built in your town. A plan of the store has been made to help you find your way around. As you look at the plan, imagine you are looking down on to the store with its roof taken off. Simple pictures called symbols show you where everything is.

Can you explain how to find the books, the toys, the shoes and the café? You need to say when to turn left or right and when to go straight on.

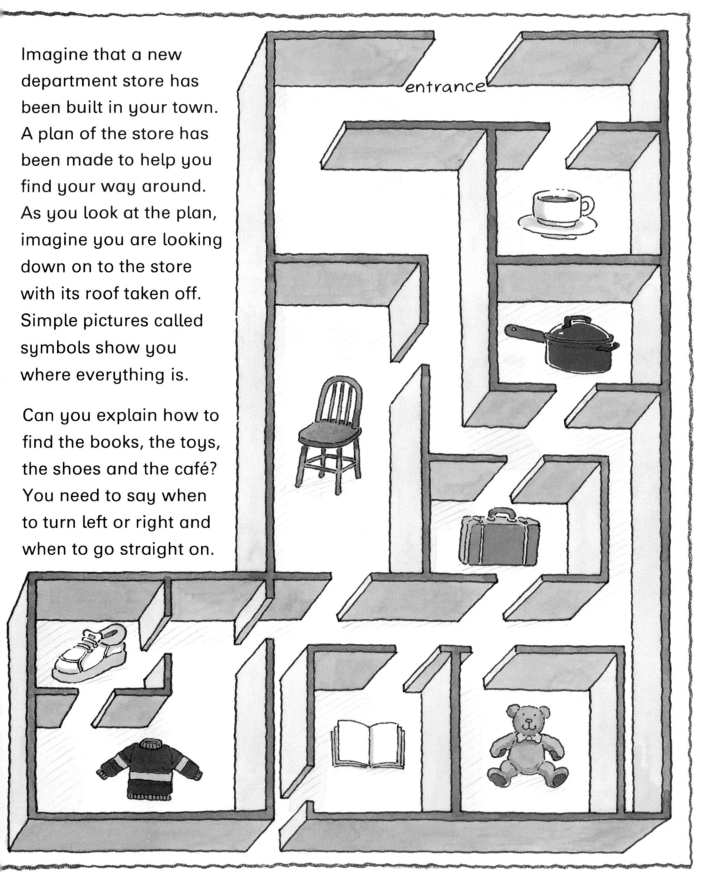

entrance

Where are shops?

Do you know the way to the shops in your local area? How far away are they? How do you get there and back?

Close your eyes and imagine the journey in your head. Then see if you can draw a picture of the route to the shops as if you were a bird looking down from the sky. This sort of picture is called a map. Make up a symbol for each kind of shop – an apple for the greengrocer's or a shoe for the shoe shop would be a good idea.

When people are choosing places to build shops, they need to think about the shape of the land and how much it costs. They also need to find a place which is near to where people live or work and which is easy to get to.

This is a plan of a new town. Imagine you are helping to plan the town. The houses and offices are already in place but the planners need to find space for the shops shown below. Where would you put each shop?

supermarket

greengrocer's

newsagent

DIY superstore

bakery

fishmonger

grocer's

Clothes shop

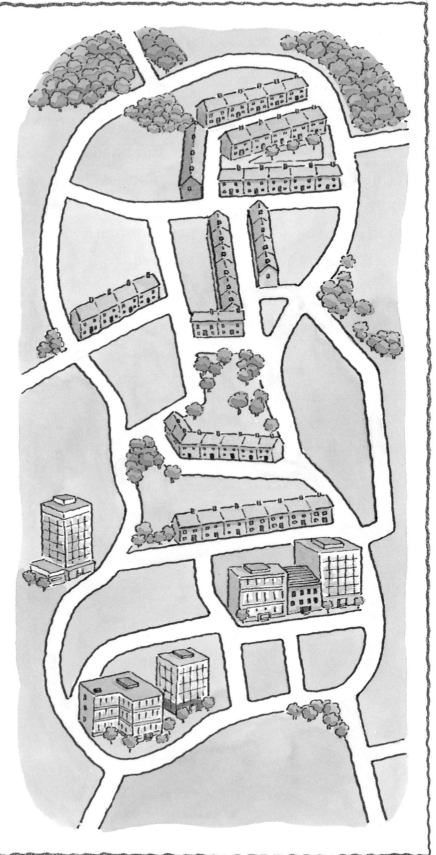

The type of shops people go to may depend on where they live. If you live in a town, there are probably lots of different shops to choose from, but the shops are often crowded and busy. If you live in the countryside, you are more likely to have just a few small shops nearby. The shops are probably quieter though, with shorter queues.

All over the world, people go shopping to buy the things they need, such as food, clothes, medicine and furniture.

Look closely at these pictures of shops in other countries. Can you see what each of the shops is selling? Do you have any shops like these near your home?

Vietnam

Malawi

Mozambique

Japan

Sri Lanka

Morocco

Goods from abroad

Look at the labels on some food packaging
at home or in your local supermarket.
How many different countries does
the food come from?

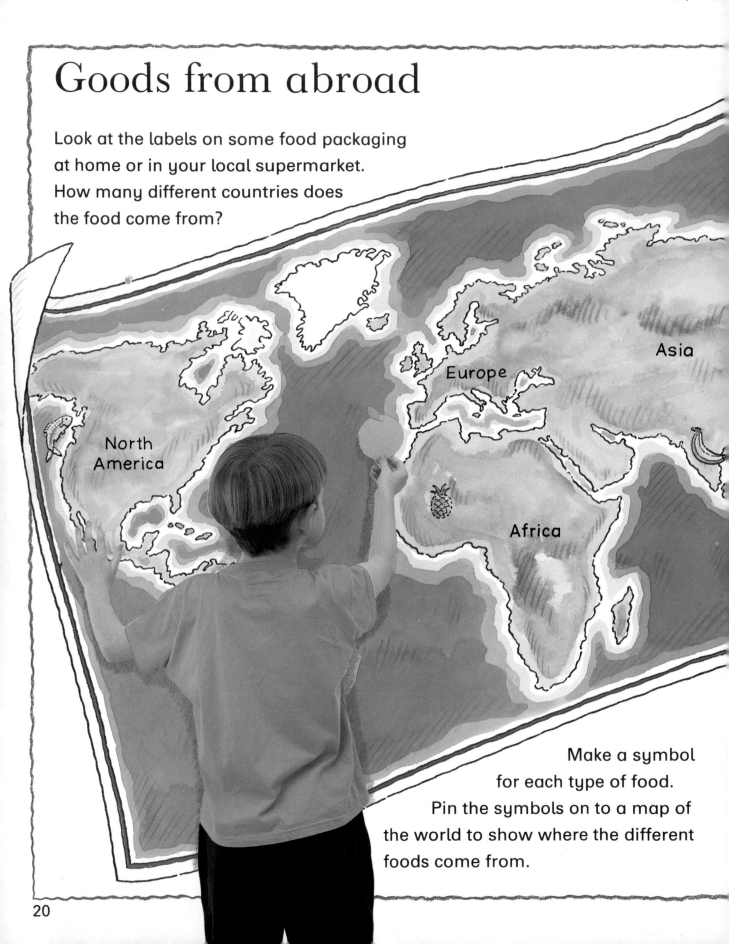

Make a symbol
for each type of food.
Pin the symbols on to a map of
the world to show where the different
foods come from.

Food has to be grown in places with the right temperature and rainfall. Each of the pictures below shows a different food being harvested in a different country. Can you find out what the climate is like in each country?

Harvesting wheat in England.

Harvesting sugar cane in the Dominican Republic.

Grape harvesting in France.

Harvesting coffee in El Salvador.

Harvesting rice in Sri Lanka.

21

When food goes on a long journey, it usually has to be prepared in a special way to stop it going off. This is called preserving.

Have a look at some food at home or in a supermarket to find out how different foods are preserved. See if you can make a chart like this one to show what you find out.

Frozen	
Tinned	
Dried	
Processed	

Some goods travel backwards and forwards across the world, visiting several countries before they are finally delivered to the shops.

See if you can plot the journey of a jumper on a map of the world.

1   Wool comes from sheep in Australia.

3   The yarn is sent to Italy to be dyed and knitted into a jumper.

2 The wool is sent to India to be spun into yarn.

4 Then the jumper is sent to the UK to be sold.

Can you find out about the journeys of some other goods, such as tea, paper, pencils or bananas?

Green shopping

Buy food with less packaging.

The journeys that goods make on their way to our shops can cause a lot of damage to the environment. Look at the journey of the jumper on page 23. How many different countries did it travel to before it arrived at a shop?

The lorries, aeroplanes and ships which transport goods across the world use up huge amounts of energy and give off dirty fumes which pollute the air.

Also, a lot of plastic and cardboard packaging is used to protect the goods on their journey. When the goods are unpacked, the packaging is thrown away.

A Colombian ship loaded with bananas.

The processes used to make many goods can also be damaging to the environment. Many products, such as clothes and paper, are made using poisonous chemicals, and many foods are sprayed with chemicals to protect them from pests and diseases while they are growing.

Reuse plastic bags.

What can you do to make shopping less damaging to the environment?

Mend clothes instead of throwing them away.

Opening a new shop

Would you like to run your own shop? What kind of things would you need to think about? You could make up a list of questions to ask your friends to find out what sort of shop they would like.

Here are some questions you could ask.

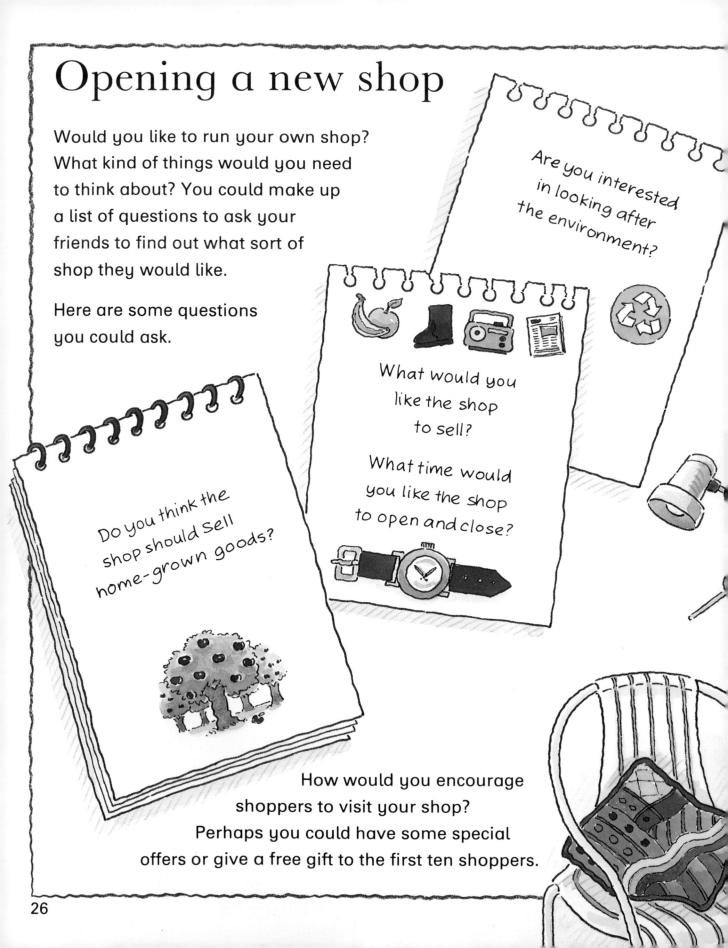

Are you interested in looking after the environment?

What would you like the shop to sell?

What time would you like the shop to open and close?

Do you think the shop should sell home-grown goods?

How would you encourage shoppers to visit your shop? Perhaps you could have some special offers or give a free gift to the first ten shoppers.

Shopping in the future

How would you like to go shopping in the future? Would you like there to be more shopping malls, where all the different shops are under one roof? Or would you like to visit one giant shop which sells everything?

Perhaps more people will shop by post from home, or use their television, telephone or computer to order goods. Would you like to shop like this?

Index

For parents and teachers
More about the ideas in this book

Pages 6/7 As well as the physical features of shops, children could also find out about the shopping behaviour and preferences of customers.

Pages 8/9 These pages introduce the principle behind shops, that of trading something you have for something else you want.

Pages 10/11 Encourage the children to find out about the history of market towns. Place names and street names can often give useful clues to the location of markets in the past.

Pages 12/13 A huge chain of people may be involved in getting goods to the shops. The amount of profit made at each link in the chain raises issues of fair trade and why some countries are poorer than others.

Pages 14/15 In a big supermarket, goods are positioned to maximise sales. For instance, expensive goods at eye level, heavy things near the entrance so customers have to take a trolley and buy more and sweets at the check-out so children will ask for them.

Pages 16/19 The location of shops depends on factors such as the economy, wealth, housing and transport in an area.

Pages 20/23 The success of an area to grow crops or rear farm animals often depends on the climate and landscape, but the processing and sale of goods depends more on skills and wealth. Children could find out about imports and exports from different countries.

Pages 24/25 Consumer pressure is an important factor in persuading shops to be 'green' traders.

Page 26 Setting up a shop presents many opportunities for market research, management skills and data handling.

Page 27 Mail order shopping was first introduced hundreds of years ago by people who lived a long way from any shops. In the future, more people are likely to shop from the comfort of their own home – perhaps in virtual reality shopping malls.

Things to do

Going places provides starting points for all kinds of cross-curricular work based on geography and the environment, both on a local and a global scale. **Where people shop** explores the origins of trade, journeys to shops, the supply of goods to communities and the impact of shopping on the environment. Here are some ideas for follow-up activities to extend the ideas further.

Making models of local shops is a useful way of focussing attention on details. What similarities or differences do the children notice? What sort of goods do the shops sell? How does the lighting, decoration or layout of a shop influence its atmosphere? Which shops do they like best? Do any of the shops have ramps or automatic doors to help elderly or disabled people or people with push chairs? How would the children improve the shops they visit?

2 Arrange for the children to interview one or more local shopkeepers about their working day. The information could be recorded in a cartoon strip or a clock diagram to illustrate 'a day in the life of a shopkeeper'.

3 Find out about Medieval markets. What sort of goods would have been sold? How much did the items cost? How long did the market last? How were crimes punished? In Medieval times, many people could not read, so market traders drew pictures to advertise their wares. The children could design their own sign for a Medieval market stall.

4 Encourage the children to find out about what shops were like years ago. Things to investigate could include the size of the shops, the range of goods, how the goods were sold, whether shops were self-service and the use of delivery bikes and vans to take goods to the customer's home.

5 Drama activities could be developed from songs or rhymes about markets or fairs – such as 'Widdecombe Fair'. The children could make up their own song or play about a visit to a local market.

6 Maths activities could include sorting or classifying shops into categories according to their size or what they sell, and carrying out surveys to compare features such as opening times, who uses the shops, the most popular items and the prices of goods. The children could also weigh or measure out specific quantities of goods and find out the cost of a few items on a shopping list.

7 Make up a mail-order catalogue in a scrapbook. Cut out pictures of things like clothes, food and toys from magazines and write a short description with the size and price underneath. Ask the children to make up a simple order form with boxes for the customers to fill in their choices.

8 Design some eye-catching posters to advertise special offers in shops.

9 Map-making activities could include journeys to the shops, journeys of goods around the world, finding out about trade routes in the past, making scale maps of the layout of shops and designing a map to guide people around an imaginary department store.

10 Encourage the children to think in more detail about the environmental issues associated with shopping, such as buying goods made from endangered species, organic farming, intensive farming, preserving food, packaging and recycling. Other environmental activities could include designing a really strong shopping bag or basket that can be used over and over again. What is the strongest and most suitable material to make the bag from?